New Testament
Activity Bible

Favorite Stories
Jesus Told

Illustrated by Bob Bond

*A Faith Building Guide
can be found on the last page*

Published in the USA by
Chariot Victor Publishing
4050 Lee Vance View
Colorado Springs
CO 80918
USA

Designed by
ANDREW MILNE DESIGN

ISBN 0-78143-318-5

Write to: John Hunt Publishing Ltd
46A West Street, Alresford, Hampshire SO24 9AU, UK

Printed in Malaysia.

CONTENTS

"Give me my share
of the property."
LUKE 15:12

THE SON LEAVES HOME

Then Jesus said, "A man had two sons. The younger son said to his father, 'Give me my share of the property.' So the father divided the property between his two sons. Then the younger son gathered up all that was his and left.

"He traveled far away to another country. There he wasted his money in foolish living. He spent everything that he had. Soon after that, the land became very dry, and there was no rain. There was not enough food to eat anywhere in the country."

WORD SEARCH

One of the words listed below is not in the word square. Which one?

Words read across, up and down and diagonally.

E	R	E	H	T	A	F	R
T	F	O	O	L	I	S	H
Y	U	S	G	H	A	J	K
P	R	O	P	E	R	T	Y
L	Z	N	X	C	M	V	R
N	E	S	F	F	O	O	D
I	D	T	H	K	N	T	O
A	R	I	W	I	E	K	K
R	J	E	O	O	Y	P	E
R	E	G	N	U	O	Y	Z

YOUNGER	FATHER	TWO
LAND	MONEY	DRY
FOOLISH	FOOD	RAIN
PROPERTY	SONS	

SPOT IN THE PICTURE

❖ The older son
❖ The younger son
❖ The father

CHECK IT OUT!

LUKE 15:11-14

DRAW A FARM

Draw five different farm animals on your farm.

BRAIN TEASER

Put the following words into the correct order.

AWAY

THE FAR

YOUNGER

TO SON

COUNTRY

TRAVELED

ANOTHER

"The son was hungry
and needed money."
LUKE 15:14

QUIZ

1 Where did the son work?

2 Who did the son feed?

3 As the son was so hungry,
what was he willing to eat?

THE SON IS STARVING

"There was not enough food to eat anywhere in the country. The son was hungry and needed money. So he got a job with one of the citizens there.

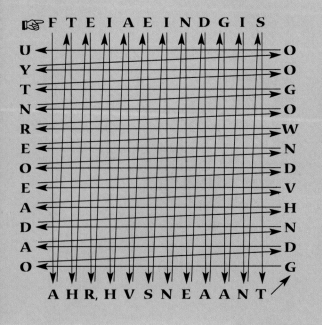

FIND THE MESSAGE

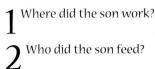

Find what the son decided he would say
to his father when he went back home.

☞ F T E I A E I N D G I S

U — O
Y — O
T — G
N — O
R — W
E — N
O — D
E — V
A — H
D — N
A — D
O — G

A H R , H V S N E A A N T

6

The man sent the son into the fields to feed pigs. The son was so hungry that he was willing to eat the food the pigs were eating. But no one gave him anything.

"The son realized that he had been very foolish. He thought, 'All of my father's servants have plenty of food. But I am here, almost dying with hunger. I will leave and return to my father. I'll say to him: Father, I have sinned against God and have done wrong to you. I am not good enough to be called your son. But let me be like one of your servants.' So the son left and went to his father."

CHECK IT OUT!
LUKE 15:14-20

BRAIN TEASER

The word "and" comes four times in the story on these pages.

Match up the pairs of "ands", and write the words linked up by "and" together on a piece of paper.

The first part of the "and" pairs	The second part of the "and" pairs
LEAVE	HAVE DONE WRONG TO YOU
SINNED AGAINST GOD	WENT
WAS HUNGRY	NEEDED MONEY
LEFT	RETURN

SPOT IN THE PICTURE

❖ The son
❖ The pigs
❖ The pigs' food

THE SPECIAL PARTY

"They began to celebrate."
LUKE 15:24

"While the son was still a long way off, his father saw him coming. He felt sorry for his son. So the father ran to him, and hugged and kissed him.

A C T I V I T Y   T I M E

BOOKMARK

Make a bookmark using the following words.

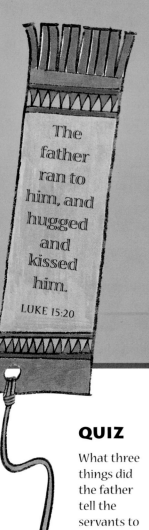

The father ran to him, and hugged and kissed him.

LUKE 15:20

QUIZ

What three things did the father tell the servants to bring his younger son?

"The son said, 'Father, I have sinned against God and have done wrong to you. I am not good enough to be called your son.'

"But the father said to his servants, 'Hurry! Bring the best clothes and put them on him. Also, put a ring on his finger and sandals on his feet. And get our fat calf and kill it. Then we can have a feast and celebrate! My son was dead, but now he is alive again! He was lost, but now he is found!'

"So they began to celebrate."

CHECK IT OUT!
LUKE 15:20-24

BRAIN TEASER

On a piece of paper write out the following sentence, filling in the missing letters. All the letters you need are consonants, that is, any letter, except A, E, I, O or U.

" - U - - - ! - - I - -
- - E - E - -
- - O - E - A - -
- U - - E - O -
- I . - A - - O,
- U - A
- I - - O - - I
- I - - E - A - -
- A - - A - S - O -
- I - - E E - . "

SPOT IN THE PICTURE

❖ The son
❖ The father
❖ Roast beef

9

THE GRUMPY SON

"The older son was angry and would not go in to the feast."
LUKE 15:28

"The older son was in the field. As he came closer to the house, he heard the sound of music and dancing. So he called to one of the servants and asked, 'What does all this mean?'

"The servant said, 'Your brother has come back. Your father killed the fat calf to eat because your brother came home safely!'

"The older son was angry and would not go in to the feast. So his father went out and begged him to come in. The son said to his father, 'I have served you like a slave for many years! I have always obeyed your commands, but you never even killed a young goat

PARTY TIME

Make a list of the ten things you like to eat at a party.

ACTIVITY TIME

QUIZ

1 Was the grumpy son:

   a: The older son?
   b: The younger son?

2 When the grumpy son came near the house what did he hear:

   a: The sound of music and dancing?
   b: The clatter of dishes being washed up?

3 The grumpy son complained to his father that he had never been given:

   a: a pig?
   b: a goat?

for me to have a feast with my friends. But your other son has wasted all your money on prostitutes. Then he comes home, and you kill the fat calf for him!'

"The father said to him, 'Son, you are always with me. All that I have is yours. We had to celebrate and be happy because your brother was dead, but now he is alive. He was lost, but now he is found.'"

CHECK IT OUT!

LUKE 15:25-32

THE MAZE

Starting at the hand, find a route through the letter maze that makes one of the sentences in the story. Follow touching letters to make the correct words. Do not go on to any square more than once. The words can be up, down, backwards, forwards or diagonal.

Write out this sentence on a piece of paper.

This leaves you with six letters that make up a word in the story. What is the word?

H	U	T	N	O
B	E	W	A	W
T	S	L	S	H
F	O	R	E	H
A	F	I	U	N
T	S	O	E	D

SPOT IN THE PICTURE

❖ The older son
❖ The father

"A farmer went out
to plant his seed."
MATTHEW 13:3

THE FARMER AND HIS SEED

Jesus went out of the house and sat by the lake. Large crowds gathered around him. So Jesus got into a boat and sat, while the people stayed on the shore. Then Jesus used stories to teach them many things.

He said: "A farmer went out to plant his seed. While he was

CLOCKWORDS

In this puzzle there are two letters in place of each number on the clock face. To make a clockword, write down the letters of the hour hand mentioned, then the letters of the minute hand mentioned. So twenty to ten equals ST OP.

On a piece of paper fill in the blanks in the following sentence, using clockwords.

---- is the ---- ---- ---- by the ----?

a: Three o'clock
b: Five past eleven
c: Twenty-five to five
d: Twenty past two
e: Half past nine

planting, some seed fell by the road. The birds came and ate all that seed." …

"So listen to the meaning of that story about the farmer.

"What is the seed that fell by the road? That seed is like the person who hears the teaching about the kingdom but does not understand it. The Evil One comes and takes away the things that were planted in that person's heart."

CHECK IT OUT!
MATTHEW 13:1-4, 18-19

U-N-J-U-M-B-L-E

"The seed gobbled up by birds stands for the kind of person who hears..."
Put the rest of this sentence in the correct order.

"...IT THE UNDERSTAND TEACHING NOT ABOUT DOES BUT THE KINGDOM"

WRONG WORDS

Spot the seven wrong words in the next two sentences, and write down or say the correct words.

JESUS WENT OUT OF THE SKY-SCRAPER AND STOOD BY THE HIGHWAY. LARGE CROWDS GATHERED AROUND HIM. SO JESUS GOT INTO A PLANE AND SAT, WHILE THE PEOPLE WAVED FROM THE GROUND.

SPOT IN THE PICTURE

❖ Boat
❖ Jesus
❖ Crowd of people
❖ Farmer

"Some seed fell on rocky ground."
MATTHEW 13:5

CHANGE ONE LETTER

In the following words, which are all from the story on these pages, change one letter to make a word.

LONEY,

THURNY,

MERSECUTION,

WURRIES,

ROCKI

U-N-J-U-M-B-L-E

a: "The seed that fell on rocky ground stands for the kind of person who hears ..."
Put the rest of this sentence in the correct order.

"... SHORT ONLY THE TIME. TEACHING A AND IT QUICKLY KEEPS ACCEPTS HE IT BUT WITH JOY."

b: "The seed that fell among thorny weeds stands for the kind of person who hears ..."
Put the rest of this sentence in the correct order.

"... TEACHING STOP BUT GROWING LETS FROM WORRIES THAT ABOUT MONEY THIS OF LIFE AND LOVE."

ROCKY GROUND AND THORNY WEEDS

Jesus said, "Some seed fell on rocky ground, where there wasn't enough soil. That seed grew very fast, because the ground was not deep. But when the sun rose, the plants dried up because they did not have deep roots.

"Some other seed fell among thorny weeds. The weeds grew and

choked the good plants....

"So listen to the meaning of that story about the farmer."...

"And what is the seed that fell on rocky ground? That seed is like the person who hears the teaching and quickly accepts it with joy. But he does not let the teaching go deep into his life. He keeps it only a short time. When trouble or persecution comes because of the teaching he accepted, then he quickly gives up.

"And what is the seed that fell among the thorny weeds? That seed is like the person who hears the teaching but lets worries about this life and love of money stop that teaching from growing. So the teaching does not produce fruit in that person's life."

CHECK IT OUT!

MATTHEW 13: 5-7, 18, 20-22

ACTIVITY TIME

GROWING CRESS

Plant some mustard and cress. Water it. Watch it grow. Make some mustard and cress sandwiches with it.

1.

2.

3.

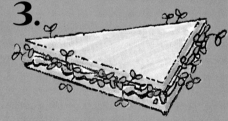

SPOT IN THE PICTURE

❖ Two seeds
❖ Rocky ground
❖ Weeds
❖ The sun

GOOD GROUND

"Some other seed
fell on good ground."
MATTHEW 13:8

U-N-J-U-M-B-L-E

"The seed that fell on good
ground stands for the kind of
person who hears ..."

Put the rest of this sentence in
the correct order.

"... **GROWS FRUIT.
THE PRODUCES
TEACHING AND AND
UNDERSTANDS
THAT PERSON IT.**"

Jesus said, "Some other seed fell on good
ground where it grew and became grain.
Some plants made 100 times more
grain. Other plants made 60 times more
grain, and some made 30 times more grain.
You people who hear me, listen!"

"So listen to the meaning of that story
about the farmer."

"But what is the seed that fell on the good ground?
That seed is like the person
who hears the teaching and
understands it. That
person grows and
produces fruit,
sometimes 100 times
more, sometimes 60
times more, and
sometimes 30 times
more."

REACH FOR YOUR CALCULATOR

a: If ten seeds were planted and
each produced 30 times more,
how many seeds grew?

b: If twenty seeds were planted
and each produced 60 times
more, how many seeds
grew?

c: If fifty seeds were
planted and each
produced 100
times more,
how many
seeds grew?

CHECK IT OUT!

MATTHEW 13:8-9, 18, 23

BRAIN TEASER

Take out the Xs to find out what happened to the fourth group of seed.

XSXOXMXE
XXOXTXHX
EXRXXSXE
XEXDXXFX
EXLXLXXO
XNXXGXOX
OXDXXGXR
XOXUXNXD
XXWXHXE
XRXEXXIX
TXXGXRXE
XWXXAXN
XDXXBXEX
CXAXXMX
EXXGXRXA
XIXNX.

SPOT IN THE PICTURE

❖ Seed
❖ Grain

17

THE ROBBERY

"They left him lying there, almost dead."
LUKE 10:30

Then a teacher of the law stood up. He was trying to test Jesus. He said, "Teacher, what must I do to get life for ever?" Jesus said to him, "What is written in the law? What do you read there?"

ACTIVITY TIME

From the letters below make up words. Five points for each word found linked to the story on these pages. One point for other words, up to a maximum of five words.:

**SOME
ROBBERS
ATTACKED
HIM**

QUIZ

1 Did the teacher of the law ask his first question:

a: to help Jesus?

b: because he really wanted to know the answer?

c: to test Jesus?

2 Was Jericho:

a: on higher ground than Jerusalem?

b: on lower ground than Jerusalem?

c: on the same level as Jerusalem?

3 Did the attack take place:

a: in the city?

b: on a track in the desert?

c: in the middle of a green field?

The man answered, "Love the Lord your God. Love him with all your heart, all your soul, all your strength, and all your mind." Also, "You must love your neighbor as you love yourself."

Jesus said to him, "Your answer is right. Do this and you will have life for ever."

But the man wanted to show that the way he was living was right. So he said to Jesus, "And who is my neighbor?"

To answer this question, Jesus said, "A man was going down the road from Jerusalem to Jericho. Some robbers attacked him. They tore off his clothes and beat him. Then they left him lying there, almost dead."

CHECK IT OUT!

LUKE 10:25-30

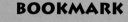

ACTIVITY TIME

BOOKMARK

Make a bookmark out of the following words:

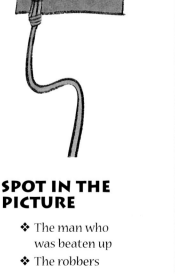

Love the Lord your God.

LUKE 10:27

SPOT IN THE PICTURE

❖ The man who was beaten up
❖ The robbers

19

THE KIND FOREIGNER

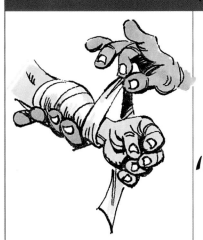

"The Samaritan took care of him."
LUKE 10:34

BRAIN TEASER

Solve the riddle written by the author of *Gulliver's Travels*, Jonathan Swift.

WE ARE LITTLE AIRY CREATURES

ALL OF DIFFERENT VOICE AND FEATURES.

ONE OF US IN GLASS IS SET,

ONE OF US YOU'LL FIND IN JET.

T'OTHER YOU MAY SEE IN TIN

AND THE FOURTH A BOX WITHIN.

IF THE FIFTH YOU SHOULD PURSUE

IT CAN NEVER FLY FROM YOU.

What are "we"?

COUNT

If you have solved the brain teaser, count the number of ----- in the story on these two pages. Ignore the letter "y".

"It happened that a Jewish priest was going down that road. When the priest saw the man, he walked by on the other side of the road.

"Next, a Levite came there. He went over and looked at the man. Then he walked by on the other side of the road.

"Then a Samaritan traveling down the road came to where the hurt man was lying. He saw the man and felt very sorry for him. The Samaritan went to him and poured olive oil and wine on his wounds and bandaged them. He put the hurt man on his own donkey and took him to an inn.

"At the inn, the Samaritan took care of him."

CHECK IT OUT!
LUKE 10:31-34

QUIZ TIME

1 Did the Jewish priest:

a: not even go and look at the hurt man?

b: go over to the hurt man, but do nothing?

c: give first aid to the hurt man?

2 Did the Levite, who helped the priests in the Temple:

a: not even go and look at the hurt man?

b: go over to the hurt man, but do nothing?

c: give first aid to the hurt man?

3 Did the Samaritan, a foreigner:

a: not even go and look at the hurt man?

b: go over to the hurt man, but do nothing?

c: give first aid to the hurt man?

SPOT IN THE PICTURE

❖ The kind Samaritan

❖ The hurt man

❖ The Samaritan's donkey

"Take care of this man."
LUKE 10:35

"GO AND DO THE SAME!"

"The next day, the Samaritan brought out two silver coins and gave them to the innkeeper. The Samaritan said, 'Take care of this man. If you spend more money on him, I will pay it back to you when I come again.'"

Then Jesus said, "Which one of these three men do you think was a neighbor to the man who was attacked by the robbers?"

DRAW

Draw your own picture of the main picture on these pages.

Include the innkeeper, the hurt man, the kind Samaritan and his donkey.

UNRAVEL

Put in the correct order.

TO THE
THE NEXT
INNKEEPER
DAY, COINS
THE AND
SAMARITAN
GAVE
BROUGHT
THEM OUT
SILVER TWO

The teacher of the law answered, "The one who helped him."

Jesus said to him, "Then go and do the same thing he did!"

CHECK IT OUT!
LUKE 10:35-37

BRAIN TEASER

Remove one circle of letters to reveal:

a: Two four letter words

b: One five letter word

c: One six letter word.

Each word starts with the letter "S" and reads from the inside of the spoke of the wheel.

All the words you need are in the story on these pages.

Ignore the letter X.

Write out these four words on a piece of paper.

```
        R
        E
        V
        L
        Q
        I
D N X E W P S A Y X I X D
        A
        Z
        M
        X
        X
        E
```

SPOT IN THE PICTURE

❖ Innkeeper

❖ Kind Samaritan

❖ Hurt man

THE RICH FOOL

"I will build bigger barns."
LUKE 12:18

BRAIN TEASER

Write out the following sentence, filling in the five missing words.

"_ _ _ _ _ _ _ MAN!
_ _ _ _ _ _ _ YOU
WILL _ _ _ .
SO WHO WILL
GET _ _ _ _ _
_ _ _ _ _ _ YOU HAVE
_ _ _ _ _ _ _ _ FOR
YOURSELF?"

WORD SEARCH

Find six words from the story on these pages. The words are up, down, across or diagonal.

B	T	Q	W	E	R	T	H
U	A	I	O	P	A	S	S
F	E	R	I	C	H	J	I
J	K	K	N	I	R	D	L
Y	E	A	R	S	Z	X	O
C	V	B	N	M	Q	O	O
P	S	D	F	G	H	J	F

Then Jesus said to them, "Be careful and guard against all kinds of greed. A man's life is not measured by the many things he owns."

Then Jesus used this story: "There was a rich man who had some land, which grew a good crop of food. The rich man thought to himself, 'What will I do? I have no place to keep all my crops'. Then he said, 'I know what I will do. I will tear down my barns and build bigger ones! I will put all my grain and other goods together in my new barns. Then I can say to myself, I have enough good things stored to last for many years. Rest, eat, drink, and enjoy life!'

"But God said to that man, 'Foolish man! Tonight you will die. So who will get those things you have prepared for yourself?'

"This is how it will be for anyone who stores things up only for himself and is not rich towards God."

CHECK IT OUT!

LUKE 12:15-21

DECODE

Remove the letters IG before each vowel and read Jesus' warning.

BIGE

CIGARIGEFIGUL

IGAND

GIGUIGARD

IGAGIGAIGINST

IGALL KIGINDS

IGOF GRIGEIGED.

The code is called "Iglish." You could use it with your friends.

SPOT IN THE PICTURE

❖ The rich man
❖ Barns
❖ Crops

25

THE PHARISEE'S PRAYER

"God, I thank You that I am not as bad as other people."
LUKE 18:11

BRAIN TEASER

Write out the following words, changing one letter in each word, to make them into words from the story on these pages.

STEEL

WEAK

MAD

TAN

DART

BENT

ANT

From the letters below make up words. Five points for each word found linked to the story on these pages. One point for other words, up to a maximum of five words.

WENT TO THE TEMPLE TO PRAY

ACTIVITY TIME

There were some people who thought that they were very good and looked down on everyone else. Jesus used this story to teach them:

"One day there was a Pharisee and a tax collector. Both went to the Temple to pray. The Pharisee stood alone, away from the tax

collector. When the Pharisee prayed, he said, 'God, I thank You that I am not as bad as other people. I am not like men who steal, cheat, or take part in adultery. I thank You that I am better than this tax collector. I give up eating twice a week, and I give one-tenth of everything I earn!'"

CHECK IT OUT!

LUKE 18: 9-12

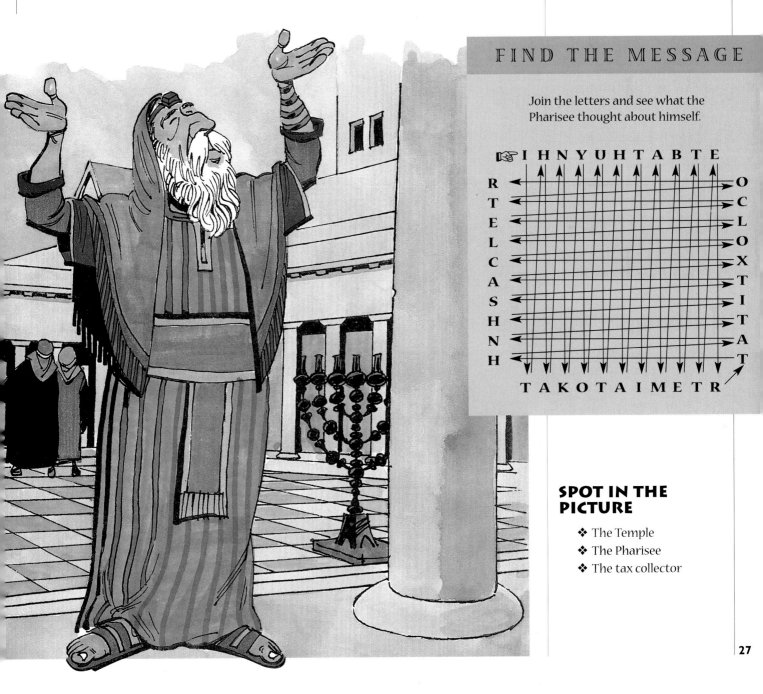

FIND THE MESSAGE

Join the letters and see what the Pharisee thought about himself.

☞ I H N Y U H T A B T E

R   O
T   C
E   C
L   L
C   O
A   X
S   T
H   I
N   T
H   A
         T

T A K O T A I M E T R

SPOT IN THE PICTURE

❖ The Temple
❖ The Pharisee
❖ The tax collector

27

THE TAX COLLECTOR'S PRAYER

"He was right with God."
LUKE 18:14

"The tax collector stood at a distance. When he prayed, he would not even look up to heaven. He beat on his chest because he was so sad.

"He said, 'God, have mercy on me. I am a sinner!'

"I tell you, when this man went home, he was right with God. But the Pharisee was not right with God. Everyone who makes himself great will be made humble. But everyone who makes himself humble will be made great."

ACTIVITY TIME

DECODE

Use the code b=a, c=b, d=c, and so on, to decode the following message:

"HPE, IBWF NFSDZ PO NF. J BN B TJOOFS!"

UNRAVEL

Put this sentence into the correct order.

LOOK
WOULD
WHEN
HEAVEN
PRAYED HE
NOT HE UP
TO EVEN

CHECK IT OUT!
LUKE 18:13-14

MULTIPLE CHOICE

1 As he prayed, the tax collector:
   a: sat down
   b: knelt down
   c: stood

2 In his prayer, the tax collector said:
   a: "I am good."
   b: "I am a sinner!"
   c: "I'm better than that Pharisee."

3 As he prayed, was the tax collector:
   a: sad?
   b: cheerful?
   c: happy?

SPOT IN THE PICTURE

❖ The Temple
❖ The tax collector
❖ The Pharisee

29

"He will look for the
lost sheep."
LUKE 15:4

THE "ONE" PUZZLE

From these twelve sticks take
away one, move two others, so
that you are left with one.

A C T I V I T Y   T I M E

DRAW

Draw your own picture of this
story with one sheep lost and
the shepherd finding it. Then
color or paint it.

SHEEP NO. 100 IS MISSING

CHECK IT OUT!

LUKE 15:3-7

Then Jesus told them this story: "Suppose one of you has 100 sheep, but he loses one of them. Then he will leave the other 99 sheep alone and go out and look for the lost sheep. The man will keep on searching for the lost sheep until he finds it. And when he finds it, the man is very happy. He puts it on his shoulders and goes home.

"He calls to his friends and neighbors and says, 'Be happy with me because I found my lost sheep!'

"In the same way, I tell you there is much joy in heaven when one sinner changes his heart. There is more joy for that one sinner than there is for 99 good people who don't need to change."

BRAIN TEASER

The computer had been programmed to sort words into alphabetical order, putting all words together beginning with a, then b, and so on. Someone forgot to turn this instruction off, so this is how a famous poem was printed.

CALM.
EVERYTHING.
GIVES. GREEN.
HAVE. HE. HE I.
I. IS. IN. LEADS.
LORD. ME. ME.
MY. NEED.
PASTURES. REST.
SHEPHERD. THE.
TO. WATER.

Here is a list of the first letters for each word. Write out the poem. Hint: Psalm 23:1.

T. L. I. M. S.
I. H. E. I. N.
H. G. M. R. I.
G. P. H. L. M.
T. C. W.

SPOT IN THE PICTURE

❖ The lost sheep
❖ The shepherd

"I have found the coin
that I lost!"
LUKE 15:9

THE LOST COIN

Many tax collectors and "sinners" came to listen to Jesus. The Pharisees and the teachers of the law began to complain: "Look! This man welcomes sinners and even eats with them!"

Then Jesus told them this story. . .

"Suppose a woman has ten silver coins, but she loses one of them. She will light a lamp and clean the house. She will look

carefully for the coin until she finds it. And when she finds it, she will call her friends and neighbors and say, 'Be happy with me because I have found the coin that I lost!' In the same way, there is joy before the angels of God when one sinner changes his heart."

CLOCKWORDS

In this puzzle there are two letters in place of each number on the clock face. To make a clockword, write down the letters of the hour hand mentioned, then the letters of the minute hand mentioned. So twenty to ten equals HE RE.

On a piece of paper fill in the blanks in the following sentence, using clockwords.

"---- **MAN WELCOMES**

SINNERS AND ---- ----

---- ----!"

a: Six o'clock

b: Ten past four

c: Five to three

d: Quarter to five

e: Twenty-five to one

CHECK IT OUT!
LUKE 15:1-3, 8-10

HIDE AND SEEK

Hide something in a room and see if someone else can find it.

Then you look for something that has been hidden.

BRAIN TEASER

Spot the six wrong words in these sentences and write out the correct words.

"SUPPOSE A GIRL HAS SIX GOLD TOYS, BUT SHE LOSES ONE OF THEM. SHE WILL LIGHT A FIRE AND CLEAN THE HOUSE. SHE WILL LOOK CAREFULLY FOR THE TOY UNTIL SHE FINDS IT."

SPOT IN THE PICTURE

❖ The lost coin
❖ The woman

"How many times
must I forgive?"
MATTHEW 18:21

BACKWARDS

Write out this sentence in the
correct order.

TIMES. 77 YOU TO
WRONG DOES HE IF
EVEN HIM FORGIVE
MUST YOU TIMES.
SEVEN THAN MORE
HIM FORGIVE MUST
YOU YOU, TELL I

THE KING COLLECTS HIS MONEY

Then Peter came to Jesus and asked, "Lord, when my brother sins against me, how many times must I forgive him? Should I forgive him as many as seven times?"

Jesus answered, "I tell you, you must forgive him more than seven times. You must forgive him even if he does wrong to you 77 times."

THE MAZE

Starting at the hand, find a route
through the letter maze that uses
six of the words in the story on
these pages. Follow touching
letters to make the correct words.
They can be up, down, backwards,
forwards or diagonal. You must not
visit any square more than once.

Write out the six words on a piece
of paper.

This leaves you with seven letters
that make up a word in the story.
What is the word?

F	V	I	K	E	N
E	O	G	Y	I	T
M	O	R	E	N	A
W	E	N	G	S	V
O	D	P	A	T	E
Y	A	M	S	R	R

"The kingdom of heaven is like a king who decided to collect the money his servants owed him. So the king began to collect his money. One servant owed him several million dollars. But the servant did not have enough money to pay his master, the king. So the master ordered that everything the servant owned should be sold, even the servant's wife and children. The money would be used to pay the king what the servant owed.

"But the servant fell on his knees and begged, 'Be patient with me. I will pay you everything I owe.' The master felt sorry for his servant. So the master told the servant he did not have to pay. He let the servant go free."

CHECK IT OUT!

MATTHEW 18:21-27

ACTIVITY TIME

BOOKMARK

Make a bookmark from the following words:

You must forgive.

MATTHEW 18:22

SPOT IN THE PICTURE

- ❖ The king
- ❖ The servant
- ❖ The servant's wife
- ❖ The servant's children

THE SERVANT COLLECTS HIS MONEY

" Pay me the money
you owe me!"
MATTHEW 18:28

"Later, that same servant found another servant who owed him a few dollars. The servant grabbed the other servant around the neck and said, 'Pay me the money you owe me!'

"The other servant fell on his knees and begged him, 'Be patient with me. I will pay you everything I owe.'

"But the first servant refused to be patient. He threw the other servant into prison until he could pay everything he owed. All the other servants saw what happened. They were very sorry. So they went and told their master all that had happened."

DECODE

Look at the symbols below each letter and then decode the sentence and see what the unforgiving servant refused to do.

A	B	C	D	E	F	G	H	I
✡	▲	✛	✓	✺	✳	◆	✿	✐

J	K	L	M	N	O	P	Q	R
✖	∽	★	❖	♠	☛	⇨	✳	☙

S	T	U	V	W	X	Y	Z
♥	✂	!	♠	◇	⁎	✴	✚

CHECK IT OUT!

MATTHEW 18:28-31

ACTIVITY TIME

ACTIVITY TIME

Find the missing word in this sentence.

"I BE EVERYTHING WITH YOU ME I PAY OWE WILL"

BRAIN TEASER

Spot the six wrong words in these sentences and write out the correct words.

"LATER, THAT SAME BOSS FOUND ANOTHER BOSS WHO GAVE HIM TRILLIONS OF CENTS."

SPOT IN THE PICTURE

❖ The servant who owed a lot of money.
❖ The servant who owed a little money.

37

THE MASTER WAS VERY ANGRY

"Then the master called his servant in and said, 'You evil servant! You begged me to forget what you owed. So I told you that you did not have to pay anything. I had mercy on you. You should have had the same mercy on that other servant.'

"Forgive from your heart."
MATTHEW 18:35

ACTIVITY TIME

Write out these words on a piece of paper, filling in the missing consonants - that is, any letters other than a, e, i, o, or u.

Hint: Matthew 5:7

- - O S   - - O
- I - E   - E - - Y
- O   O - - E - S
A - E   - A - - Y.
- E - - Y   - I - -
- E   - I - E -
- O   - - E - .

QUIZ

1 How much money did the first servant owe:

a: a few dollars?

b: millions of dollars?

2 How much money did the second servant owe:

a: a few dollars?

b: millions of dollars?

3 How many times did Jesus tell Peter to forgive:

a: 7 times?

b: 77 times?

"The master was very angry, and he put the servant in prison to be punished. The servant had to stay in prison until he could pay everything he owed.

"This king did what my heavenly Father will do to you if you do not forgive your brother from your heart."

CHECK IT OUT!

MATTHEW 18:32-35

DECODE

Remove the letters AP before each vowel and find out what the servant should have done.

**API HAPAD
MAPERCY
APON
YAPOAPU.
YAPOAPU
SHAPOAPULD
HAPAVAPE
HAPAD THAPE
SAPAMAPE
MAPERCY
APON THAPAT
APOTHAPER
SAPERVAPANT.**

This code is called "Apish." You could use it with your friends.

SPOT IN THE PICTURE

❖ The unforgiving servant
❖ The king

THE GREAT FEAST

"Come! Everything is ready!"
LUKE 14:17

One of the men sitting at the table with Jesus heard these things. The man said to Jesus, "The people who will eat a meal in God's kingdom are blessed."

Jesus said to him, "A man gave a big banquet and invited many people. When it was time to eat, the man sent his servant to tell the guests, 'Come! Everything is ready!'

"But all the guests said they could not come. Each man made an excuse. The first one said, 'I have just bought a field, and I must go and look at it. Please excuse me.'

"Another man said, 'I have just bought five pairs of oxen; I must go and try them. Please excuse me.'

"A third man said, 'I just got married; I can't come.'"

FACT FILE

What do the letters R.S.V.P. stand for on an invitation?

What is the English version?

RS
V
P

MAKE A LIST

What are the ten best things you like to do at a party?

CHECK IT OUT!
LUKE 14:15-20

QUIZ

1 What was the first man's excuse? I can't come:

a: "I must go and look at my new field."

b: "I must go and sail my new boat."

c: "I must give my new car a run."

2 What was the second man's excuse: I can't come:

a: "I've just bought a kitten."

b: "I've just bought five pairs of oxen."

c: "I've just bought a flock of sheep."

3 What was the third man's excuse: I can't come:

a: "My wife's just had a baby."

b: "My mother is ill."

c: "I've just got married."

SPOT IN THE PICTURE

❖ The man who is giving the party

❖ Party food.

FREE!

"Bring in the poor."
LUKE 14:21

BRAIN TEASER

I OCCUR ONCE IN EVERY MINUTE, TWICE IN EVERY MOMENT, BUT NOT ONCE IN A HUNDRED THOUSAND YEARS.

What am I?

COUNT

In the Bible story printed on these pages count the number of things that are the answer to the Brain Teaser.

A PARTY FOR EVERYONE

"So the servant returned. He told his master what had happened. Then the master became angry and said, 'Go at once into the streets and alleys of the town. Bring in the poor, the crippled, the blind, and the lame.'

"Later the servant said to him,
'Master, I did what you told me to do, but
we still have places for more people.'

"The master said to the servant,
'Go out to the roads and country lanes.
Tell the people there to come. I want
my house to be full! None of those
men that I invited first will
ever eat with me!'"

CHECK IT OUT!
LUKE 14:21-24

FIND THE MESSAGE

Find out the instructions the man
organizing the party gave to his servant.

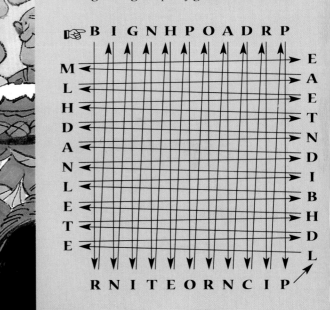

☞ B I G N H P O A D R P

M L H D A N L E T E

E A E T N D I B H D L

R N I T E O R N C I P

SPOT IN THE PICTURE

❖ The man organizing
the party.
❖ A blind person
❖ A poor person
❖ A crippled person

THE SHEEP AND THE GOATS

"He will separate them into two groups."
MATTHEW 25:32

Jesus said, "The Son of Man will come again in His great glory. All His angels will come with Him. He will be King and sit on His great throne. All the people of the world will be gathered before Him. Then He will separate them into two groups as a shepherd separates the sheep from the goats. The Son of Man will put the

QUIZ

1 Are the sheep:

a: on the right hand side of the King?
b: on the left hand side of the King?

2 Do the goats stand for:
a: good people?
b: bad people?

FACT FILE

1 Sheep and goats used to be in the same fields with each other.
a: True
b: False

2 Tents used to be made out of goat's hair.
a: True
b: False

3 Making clothes out of sheep's wool is a modern invention.
a: True
b: False

sheep, the good people, on His right and the goats, the bad people, on His left.

"Then the King will say to the good people on His right, 'Come. My Father has given you His blessing. Come and receive the kingdom God has prepared for you since the world was made. I was hungry, and you gave Me food. I was thirsty, and you gave Me something to drink. I was alone and away from home, and you invited Me into your house. I was without clothes, and you gave Me something to wear. I was sick, and you cared for Me. I was in prison, and you visited Me.'"

CHECK IT OUT!
MATTHEW 25:31-36

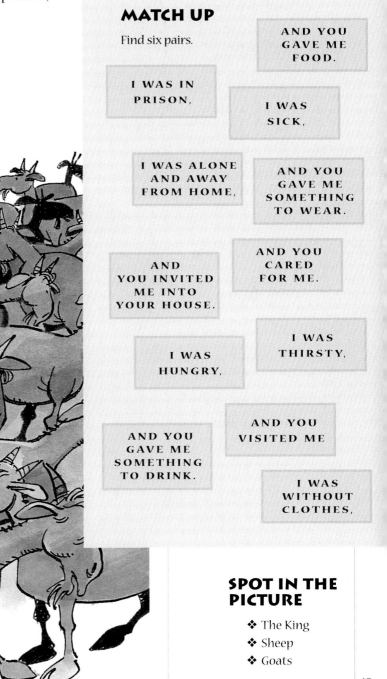

MATCH UP

Find six pairs.

AND YOU GAVE ME FOOD.

I WAS IN PRISON,

I WAS SICK,

I WAS ALONE AND AWAY FROM HOME,

AND YOU GAVE ME SOMETHING TO WEAR.

AND YOU INVITED ME INTO YOUR HOUSE.

AND YOU CARED FOR ME.

I WAS HUNGRY,

I WAS THIRSTY,

AND YOU GAVE ME SOMETHING TO DRINK.

AND YOU VISITED ME

I WAS WITHOUT CLOTHES,

SPOT IN THE PICTURE

❖ The King
❖ Sheep
❖ Goats

45

"You did [it] for me."
MATTHEW 25:40

BRAIN TEASER

On a piece of paper write out six words from below. They all come in the story on these two pages.

E O C H L T S;
U G H N R Y;
I H R S T T Y;
I O N P R S;
I O U H T T W;
E I I N T V.

UNRAVEL

On a piece of paper write out in the correct order:

YOU
ANYTHING
ALSO YOU
DID DID
FOR FOR
ANY OF ME
MY HERE
PEOPLE

CARING FOR PEOPLE

"Then the good people will answer, 'Lord, when did we see You thungry and give You food? When did we see You thirsty and give You something to drink? When did we see You alone and away from home and invite You into our house? When did we see You without clothes and give You something to wear? When did we see You sick or in prison and care for You?'

"Then the King will answer, 'I tell you the truth. Anything you did for any of My people here, you also did for Me.'"

CHECK IT OUT!

MATTHEW 25:37-40

DRAW

Draw and color in, or paint any kind act from today's story.

FACT FILE

Goats were black; **sheep** were white.

Goats were driven by a shepherd;, **sheep** followed the shepherd.

Goats were destructive eating everything green and growing; **sheep** prefer grass.

A **lamb** was often a much loved family pet, even sleeping with the children.

SPOT IN THE PICTURE

❖ A hungry person being given food.

❖ A thirsty person being given drink.

NOT HELPING PEOPLE

"You gave me nothing to eat."
MATTHEW 25:42

MAKE A MOTTO

On a very large piece of paper write out and decorate the following motto.

"Good people will live for ever."
MATTHEW 25:46

"Then the King will say to those on his left, 'Go away from Me. God has said that you will be punished. Go into the fire that burns for ever. That fire was prepared for the devil and his helpers. I was hungry, and you gave Me nothing to eat. I was thirsty, and you gave Me nothing to drink. I was alone and away from home, and you did not invite Me into your house. I was without clothes, and you gave Me nothing to wear. I was sick and in prison, and you did not care for Me.'

"Then those people will answer, 'Lord, when did we see You hungry or thirsty? When did we see You alone and away from home? Or when did we see You without clothes or sick or in prison? When did we see these things and not help You?'

"Then the King will answer, 'I tell you the truth. Anything you refused to do for any of My people here, you refused to do for Me.'

"These people will go off to be punished for ever. But the good people will go to live for ever."

CHECK IT OUT!

MATTHEW 25:41-46

WORD SEARCH

Find a sentence in the word search from the story on these pages.

That will leave you with five letters. From them make up a word also from the story.

I	S	R	E	M	E
T	W	I	H	V	N
Y	A	A	T	A	O
N	D	A	S	G	T
E	T	Y	O	U	H
L	O	G	N	I	O
N	D	R	I	N	K

MAKE A LIST

Make a list of five kind actions that have happened to you or that you have been able to help other people with.

SPOT IN THE PICTURE

❖ The King
❖ Good people
❖ Bad people

DIGGING A HOLE

"He hid his master's money in the hole."
MATTHEW 25:18

BRAIN TEASER

With the story on these pages in mind, which is the odd one out?

ONE, TWO, FIVE, NINE.

CORRECT

There are ten mistakes to spot in the following sentences.

HE GAVE ONE SERVANT SIX BAGS OF GOLD. HE GAVE ANOTHER SERVANT THREE BAGS OF SILVER. AND HE GAVE A FOURTH FRIEND FOUR POTS OF HONEY. THEN THE MAN SNEEZED.

Jesus said, "The kingdom of heaven is like a man who was going to another place for a visit. Before he left, he talked with his servants. The man told them to take care of his things while he was gone. He decided how much each servant would be able to care for. He gave one servant five bags of money. He gave another servant two bags of money. And he gave a third servant one bag of money. Then the man left.

"The servant who got five bags went quickly to invest the money. The five bags of money earned five more. It was the same with the servant who had two bags of money. He invested the money and earned two more. But the servant who got one bag of money went out and dug a hole in the ground. Then he hid his master's money in the hole."

CHECK IT OUT!

MATTHEW 25:14-18

DECODE

Remove the letters OY before each vowel and find out what the third servant did with his money.

BOYUT THOYE SOYERVOYANT WHOYO GOYOT OYONE BOYAG OYOF MOYONOYEY WOYENT OYOOYUT OYAND DOYUG OYA HOYOLOYE OYIN THOYE GROYOOYUND.

This code is called "Oyrish." You could use it with your friends.

SPOT IN THE PICTURE

- ❖ A camel.
- ❖ The man who gave his servants bags of money.
- ❖ One bag of money.
- ❖ Two bags of money.
- ❖ Five bags of money.
- ❖ A hole in the ground.

WELL DONE!

"You did well."
MATTHEW 25:21

BRAIN TEASER

Spot all the differences between what the master said to the first servant, and what he said to the second servant.

Hint: trick question.

REACH FOR YOUR CALCULATOR

a: Add up all the numbers that come in the story on these two pages. What is the total?

b: How many bags of money did the first servant bring to the master?

c: How many bags of money did the second servant bring to the master?

Jesus continued, "After a long time the master came home. He asked the servants what they did with his money. The servant who got five bags of money brought five more bags to the master. The servant said, 'Master, you trusted me to care for five bags of money. So I used your five bags to earn five more.'

"The master answered, 'You did well. You are a good servant who can be trusted. You did well with small things. So I will let you care for much greater things. Come and share my happiness with me.'

"Then the servant who got two bags of money came to the master. The servant said, 'Master, you gave me two bags of money to care for. So I used your two bags to earn two more.'

"The master answered, 'You did well. You are a good servant who can be trusted. You did well with small things. So I will let you care for much greater things. Come and share my happiness with me.'"

CHECK IT OUT!

MATTHEW 25:19-23

WHO'S WHO?

In this story each person stands for somebody.

1 The master stands for:
   a: Your teacher
   b: God

2 The bags of money stand for:
   a: The talents God has given to everyone
   b: Stolen treasure

3 The servants stand for:
   a: All adults and boys and girls
   b: People from Mars

SPOT IN THE PICTURE

❖ The master
❖ The servant with four bags of money
❖ The servant with ten bags of money

USE YOUR GIFTS

"You are a bad and
lazy servant!"
MATTHEW 25:26

Jesus continued, "Then the servant who got one bag of money came to the master. The servant said, 'Master, I knew that you were a hard man. You harvest things you did not plant. You gather crops where you did not sow any seed. So I was afraid. I went and hid your money in the ground. Here is the bag of money you gave me.'

"The master answered, 'You are a bad and lazy servant! You say you knew that I harvest things I did not plant, and that I gather crops where I did not sow any seed? So you should have put my money

BRAIN TEASER

What are the six words?

DLUOHS   RETSAM   REHTAF

DIARFA   ELPOEP   DNUORG

MAKE A LIST

Make a list of ten gifts God has given you.

in the bank. Then, when I came home, I would get my money back with interest.'

"So the master told his other servants, 'Take the bag of money from that servant and give it to the servant who has ten bags of money. Everyone who uses what he has will get more. He will have much more than he needs. But the one who does not use what he has will have everything taken away from him.'

"Then the master said, 'Throw that useless servant outside, into the darkness! There people will cry and grind their teeth with pain.'"

CHECK IT OUT!

MATTHEW 25:24-30

ACTIVITY TIME

MAKING WORDS

From the letters below make up words. Five points for each word found linked to the story on these pages. One point for other words, up to a maximum of five words.

I WOULD GET MY MONEY BACK WITH INTEREST

SPOT IN THE PICTURE

- ❖ The master
- ❖ The servant with 4 bags of money
- ❖ The servant with 10 bags of money
- ❖ The servant with a bag of money

KEEP ON PRAYING

"Lord, please teach us
how to pray."
LUKE 11:1

O nce Jesus was praying in a place. When He had finished, one of his followers said to Him, "John taught his followers how to pray. Lord, please teach us how to pray, too."

Jesus said to them, "When you pray, say:
'Father, we pray that Your name will always be kept holy.
We pray that Your kingdom will come.

Give us the food we need for each day.

Forgive us the sins we have done, because we forgive every person who has done wrong to us.

And do not cause us to be tested.'"

Then Jesus said to them, "Suppose one of you went to your friend's house at midnight and said to him, 'A friend of mine has come into town to visit me, but I have nothing for him to eat. Please lend me three loaves of bread.'

"Your friend inside the house answers, 'Don't bother me! The door is already locked. My children and I are in bed. I cannot get up and give you the bread now.'

"I tell you, perhaps friendship is not enough to make him get up to give you the bread. But he will surely get up to give you what you need if you continue to ask. So I tell you, continue to ask, and God will give to you. Continue to search, and you will find. Continue to knock, and the door will open for you. Yes, if a person continues asking, he will receive. If he continues searching, he will find. And if he continues knocking, the door will open for him."

CLOCKWORDS

In this puzzle there are two letters in place of each number on the clock face. To make a clockword, write down the letters of the hour hand mentioned, then the letters of the minute hand mentioned. So twenty to ten equals BO LD.

Hint: the words come in the most famous Christian prayer.

On a piece of paper write out the words.

  a: Four o'clock
  b: Ten past three
  c: Five to nine
  d: Five past five
  e: Twenty-five to six

ACTIVITY TIME

CHECK IT OUT!

LUKE 11:1-10

MAKE A POSTER

Make a poster from one sentence of the Lord's Prayer. Choose the one you like best. Use the version of the Lord's Prayer you know. Color in the words.

BRAIN TEASER

Spot the eight mistakes in the following sentences. On a piece of paper write out the correct words.

CONTINUE TO GRUMBLE, AND GOD WILL GIVE TO YOU. START TO LOOK AND YOU WILL SEE. CONTINUE TO HAMMER, AND THE WINDOW WILL SHUT FOR YOU.

SPOT IN THE PICTURE

❖ Man who has no food for his guests.

THE RICH MAN AND LAZARUS

"A rich man dressed in the finest clothes."
LUKE 16:19

Jesus said, "There was a rich man who always dressed in the finest clothes. He lived in luxury every day. There was also a very poor man named Lazarus, whose body was covered with sores. Lazarus was often placed at the rich man's gate. He wanted to eat only the small pieces of food that fell from the rich man's table. And the dogs would come and lick his sores!

BRAIN TEASER

Write out in the correct order.

FOOD HE RICH WANTED THAT TO FELL EAT FROM ONLY THE THE MAN'S SMALL TABLE PIECES OF.

QUIZ

1 What was the name of the poor man:
  a: Thomas?
  b: Lazarus?

2 What was the name of the rich man: (hint: beware, this is a trick question!)
  a: Matthew?
  b: Paul?

"Later, Lazarus died. The angels took Lazarus and placed him in the arms of Abraham.

"The rich man died, too, and was buried. But he was sent to where the dead are and had much pain.

"The rich man saw Abraham far away with Lazarus in his arms. He called, 'Father Abraham, have mercy on me! Send Lazarus to me so that he can dip his finger in water and cool my tongue.'"

CHECK IT OUT!

LUKE 16:19-24

FACT FILE

Some people when they talk about this story, call the rich man Dives. Dives means "rich man" in Greek. Greek was the language the New Testament was first written in.

DRAW

Draw a picture of the poor man and the very rich man.

Color, or paint it.

SPOT IN THE PICTURE

❖ The rich man
❖ The poor man
❖ A dog

LISTENING TO GOD

"I have five brothers."
LUKE 16:28

Jesus continued, "But Abraham said, 'My child, remember when you lived? You had all the good things in life, but all the bad things happened to Lazarus. Now Lazarus is comforted here, and you are suffering. Also, there is a big pit between you and us. No one can cross over to help you. And no one can leave there and come here.'

"The rich man said, 'Then please send Lazarus to my father's house on earth! I have five brothers. Lazarus could warn my brothers so that they will not come to this place of pain.'

"But Abraham said, 'They have the law of Moses and the writings of the prophets to read; let them learn from them!'

"The rich man said, 'No, father Abraham! If someone came to them from the dead, they would believe and change their hearts and lives.'

"But Abraham said to him, 'No! If your brothers won't listen to Moses and the prophets, then they won't listen to someone who comes back from death.'"

WORD SEARCH

Find part of a sentence in the word search from the story on these pages.

That will leave you with seven letters. From them make up a word also from the story.

T	W	A	E	T	E
O	H	L	H	V	A
F	M	E	A	B	A
O	T	R	Y	H	A
D	S	H	T	I	N
E	N	I	E	M	G
A	S	R	W	H	S

BRAIN TEASER

The words below are all from the story on these two pages. They all have one thing in common. None of the other words in the story share this thing. What is it?

IN, AND, CAN, ON

CHECK IT OUT!

LUKE 16:25-31

FACT FILE

Abraham lived about 1,800 years before Jesus. He was the "father" that is, the founder of the Jewish nation. He is alive now, in heaven.

QUIZ

a: How many brothers did the rich man have?

b: What should the brothers have listened to?

SPOT IN THE PICTURE

- ❖ The five brothers
- ❖ Bonfire

ANSWERS

PAGES 4-5

WORD SEARCH

Ten points for seeing that the word not in the word search is LAND.

SPOT IN THE PICTURE

One point for finding each of the things asked for.

CHECK IT OUT!

Five points for reading this, or listening as it is read to you.

DRAW

Five points for drawing a farm. One extra point for each animal, up to a maximum of five points.

BRAIN TEASER

The younger son traveled far away to another country.

Five points for correct order.

Record your total score for pages 4-5.

PAGES 6-7

QUIZ

1: In the fields.

2: Pigs.

3: The food the pigs were eating.

Three points for each correct answer.

FIND THE MESSAGE

'Father, I have sinned against God and have done wrong to you.'

Five points.

CHECK IT OUT!

Five points for reading this, or listening as it is read to you.

BRAIN TEASER

'leave' goes with 'return'

'was hungry' goes with 'needed money'

'sinned against God' goes with 'have done wrong to you'

'left' goes with 'went'

Two points for each correct match up.

SPOT IN THE PICTURE

One point for finding each of the things asked for.

Record your total score for pages 6-7.

PAGES 8-9

BOOKMARK

Ten points

QUIZ

Best clothes, a ring, sandals.

Three points for each correct answer.

CHECK IT OUT!

Five points for reading this, or listening as it is read to you.

BRAIN TEASER

'Hurry! Bring the best clothes and put them on him. Also, put a ring on his finger and sandals on his feet.'

Two points for each correct word.

SPOT IN THE PICTURE

One point for finding each of the things asked for.

Record your total score for pages 8-9.

PAGES 10-11

ACTIVITY TIME

One point for each thing on your list, up to ten points.

QUIZ

1a; 2a; 3b

Three points for each correct answer.

CHECK IT OUT!

Five points for reading this, or listening as it is read to you.

THE MAZE

'He was lost, but now he is found.' The six letters left make the word 'father'.

Ten points for completing your way through the maze.

Five points for writing out the sentence correctly.

Five points for finding the word 'father'.

SPOT IN THE PICTURE

One point for finding each of the things asked for.

Record your total score for pages 10-11.

Add up and record your total score for the story of the boy who left home.

PAGES 12-13

CLOCKWORDS

a: WHAT

b: SEED

c: THAT

d: FELL

e: ROAD

What is the seed that fell by the road? Three points for each correct word.

CHECK IT OUT!

Five points for reading this, or listening as it is read to you.

U-N-J-U-M-B-L-E

the teaching about the kingdom but does not understand it.

Five points for putting in the correct order.

WRONG WORDS

Jesus went out of the **house** and **sat** by the **lake**. Large crowds gathered around him. So Jesus got into a **boat** and **sat**, while the people **stayed on** the **shore**.

One point for each word you replace with the correct word.

SPOT IN THE PICTURE

One point for finding each of the things asked for.

Record your total score for pages 12-13.

PAGES 14-15

CHANGE ONE LETTER

Money, thorny, persecution, worries, rocky.

One point for each correct word.

U-N-J-U-M-B-L-E

a: the teaching and quickly accepts it with joy. But he keeps it only a short time.

Five points for putting in the correct order.

b: but lets worries about this life and love of money stop that teaching from growing.

Five points for putting in the correct order.

CHECK IT OUT!

Five points for reading this, or listening as it is read to you.

ACTIVITY TIME

Five points for planting mustard and cress.

Five points for watering it.

Five points for helping to make sandwiches with it.

SPOT IN THE PICTURE

One point for finding each of the things asked for.

Record your total score for pages 14-15.

PAGES 16-17

U-N-J-U-M-B-L-E

the teaching and understands it. That person grows and produces fruit.

Five points for putting in the correct order.

REACH FOR YOUR CALCULATOR

a: 300 seeds; b: 1,200 seeds; c: 5,000 seeds.

Three points for each correct answer.

CHECK IT OUT!

Five points for reading this, or listening as it is read to you.

BRAIN TEASER

Some other seed fell on good ground where it grew and became grain.

Two points for each correct word.

SPOT IN THE PICTURE

One point for finding each of the things asked for.

Record your total score for pages 16-17.

Add up and record your total score for the story of what happened to the farmer's seed.

PAGES 18-19

QUIZ

1c; 2b; 3b

Three points for each correct answer.

BOOKMARK

Ten points.

ACTIVITY TIME

Words linked to the story, like 'road' five points each. Other words, one point each, up to a maximum of five words.

SPOT IN THE PICTURE

One point for finding each of the things asked for.

CHECK IT OUT!

Five points for reading this, or listening as it is read to you.

Record your total score for pages 18-19.

PAGES 20-21

BRAIN TEASER

Vowels, the letters a, e, i, o, u.

Ten points.

COUNT

164

Ten points.

CHECK IT OUT!

Five points for reading this, or listening as it is read to you.

QUIZ

1a; 2b; 3c

Three points for each correct answer.

SPOT IN THE PICTURE

One point for finding each of the things asked for.

Record your total score for pages 20-21.

PAGES 22-23

DRAW

Five points for your drawing. Five more points for including the things asked for.

UNRAVEL

"The next day, the Samaritan brought out two silver coins and gave them to the innkeeper."
Five points

CHECK IT OUT!

Five points for reading this, or listening as it is read to you.

BRAIN TEASER

a: Said; same
b: Spend
c: Silver
Remove the circle with the letters Q, Y, Z and W in it.
Three points for each correct word.

SPOT IN THE PICTURE

One point for finding each of the things asked for.

Record your total score for pages 22-23.

Add up and record your total score for the story of the man who was beaten up.

PAGES 24-25

BRAIN TEASER

"Foolish man! Tonight you will die. So who will get those things you have prepared for yourself?"
Two points for each correct word.

WORD SEARCH

Years, foolish, rich, barns, eat, drink.
One point for each correct word.

CHECK IT OUT!

Five points for reading this, or listening as it is read to you.

DECODE

"Be careful and guard against all kinds of greed."
Two points for each correct word.

SPOT IN THE PICTURE

One point for finding each of the things asked for.

Record your total score for pages 24-25

PAGES 26-27

BRAIN TEASER

Steal, week, bad, tax, part, went, and
Two points for each correct word.

ACTIVITY TIME

Words linked to the story, like "men" five points each. Other words, one point each, up to a maximum of five words.

CHECK IT OUT!

Five points for reading this, or listening as it is read to you.

FIND THE MESSAGE

I thank you that I am better than this tax collector.
Two points for each correct word.

SPOT IN THE PICTURE

One point for finding each of the things asked for.

Record your total score for pages 26-27

PAGES 28-29

DECODE

"God, have mercy on me. I am a sinner!"

UNRAVEL

When he prayed, he would not even look up to heaven.

CHECK IT OUT!

Five points for reading this, or listening as it is read to you.

MULTIPLE CHOICE

1c; 2b; 3a

SPOT IN THE PICTURE

One point for finding each of the things asked for.

Record your total score for pages 28-29

Add up and record your total score for the story about two ways to pray.

PAGES 30-31

THE "ONE" PUZZLE

From the second square of four matchsticks take away the top horizontal one; move the bottom horizontal one so it links the top of the left hand match with the bottom of the right hand match. From the third square of four matchsticks move the right hand upright match and place it to form the letter 'E' by putting it between the two existing horizontal matches, with one of its ends resting against the middle of the left hand upright match. this gives you three letters: 'ONE'
Fifteen points for doing this.

DRAW

Ten points

CHECK IT OUT!

Five points for reading this, or listening as it is read to you.

BRAIN TEASER

The Lord is my Shepherd.
I have everything I need.
He gives me rest in green pastures.
He leads me to calm water.
Psalm 23:1
Ten points

SPOT IN THE PICTURE

One point for finding each of the things asked for.

Record your total score for pages 30-31.

PAGES 32-33

CLOCKWORDS

"This man welcomes sinners and even eats with them!"
a: THIS b: EVEN
c: EATS d: WITH e: THEM
Three points for each correct word.

CHECK IT OUT!

Five points for reading this, or listening as it is read to you.

HIDE AND SEEK

Ten points.

BRAIN TEASER

"Suppose a **woman** has **ten silver coins**, but she loses one of them. She will light a **lamp** and clean the house. She will look carefully for the **coin** until she finds it."
One point for each correct word.

SPOT IN THE PICTURE

One point for finding each of the things asked for.

Record your total score for pages 32-33.

PAGES 34-35

BACKWARDS

"I tell you, you must forgive him more than seven times. You must forgive him even if he does wrong to you 77 times."
Five points.

THE MAZE

Forgive, money, king, pay, owed, master.
Two points for each word.
Servant.
Five points.

CHECK IT OUT!

Five points for reading this, or listening as it is read to you.

Record your total score for pages 34-35.

BOOKMARK

Ten points.

SPOT IN THE PICTURE

One point for finding each of the things asked for.

PAGES 36-37

DECODE

The first servant refused to be patient.
Two points for each word.

CHECK IT OUT!

Five points for reading this, or listening as it is read to you.

ACTIVITY TIME

"Be patient with me. I will pay you everything I owe."
Patient
Five points.

BRAIN TEASER

"Later, that same **servant** found another **servant** who **owed** him **a few dollars**."
One point for each correct word.

SPOT IN THE PICTURE

One point for finding each of the things asked for.

Record your total score for pages 36-37.

PAGES 38-39

ACTIVITY TIME

Those who give mercy to others are happy.
Mercy will be given to them.
One point for each word.

QUIZ

1b; 2a; 3b
Three points for each correct answer.

CHECK IT OUT!

Five points for reading this, or listening as it is read to you.

DECODE

I had mercy on you. You should have had the same mercy on that other servant.
One point for each word.

SPOT IN THE PICTURE

One point for finding each of the things asked for.

Record your total score for pages 38-39.

Add up and record your total score for the story of the unforgiving servant.

PAGES 40-41

MAKE A LIST

One point for each thing on your list, up to ten points.

FACT FILE

Répondez s'il vous plait
Reply if pleases you: please reply.
Seven points for the French.
Three points for the English.

CHECK IT OUT!

Five points for reading this, or listening as it is read to you.

QUIZ

1a; 2b; 3c

SPOT IN THE PICTURE

One point for finding each of the things asked for.

Record your total score for pages 40-41.

PAGES 42-43

BRAIN TEASER

The letter m.
Five points.

COUNT

13
Five points.

CHECK IT OUT!

Five points for reading this, or

listening as it is read to you.

FIND THE MESSAGE
Bring in the poor, and crippled, the blind, and the lame.
Two points for each correct word.

SPOT IN THE PICTURE
One point for finding each of the things asked for.

Record your total score for pages 42-43.

Add up and record your total score for the story of the great party.

PAGES 44-45

QUIZ
1a; 2b
Three points for each correct answer.

FACT FILE
1a; 2a; 3b
Three points for each correct answer.

CHECK IT OUT!
Five points for reading this, or listening as it is read to you.

MATCH UP
I was hungry, MATCHES WITH and you gave me food.
I was thirsty, MATCHES WITH and you gave me something to drink.
I was alone and away from home, MATCHES WITH and you invited me into your house.
I was without clothes, MATCHES WITH and you gave me something to wear.
I was sick, MATCHES WITH and you cared for me.
I was in prison, MATCHES WITH and you visited me
Two points for each pair you correctly matched up.

SPOT IN THE PICTURE
One point for finding each of the things asked for.

Record your total score for pages 44-45.

PAGES 46-47

BRAIN TEASER
Clothes; hungry; thirsty; prison; without; invite.
Two points for each correct word.

UNRAVEL
Anything you did for any of my people here, you also did for me.
Five points for correct order.

CHECK IT OUT!
Five points for reading this, or listening as it is read to you.

DRAW
Five points for drawing.
Five points for coloring in.

SPOT IN THE PICTURE
One point for finding each of the things asked for.

Record your total score for pages 46-47.

PAGES 48-49

MAKE A MOTTO
Ten points.

CHECK IT OUT!
Five points for reading this, or listening as it is read to you.

WORD SEARCH
I was thirsty, and you gave me nothing to drink.
One point for each word.
Alone.
Three points.

MAKE A LIST
One point for each thing on your list, up to five points.

SPOT IN THE PICTURE
One point for finding each of the things asked for.

Record your total score for pages 48-49.

Add up and record your total score for the story of the sheep and the goats.

PAGES 50-51

BRAIN TEASER
Nine. Nine is the only number not mentioned in the story.
Three points.

CORRECT
He gave one servant **five** bags of **money**. He gave another servant **two** bags of **money**. And he gave a **third** servant **one bag** of **money**. Then the man **left**.
One point for each correct word.

CHECK IT OUT!
Five points for reading this, or listening as it is read to you.

DECODE
But the servant who got one bag of money went out and dug a hole in the ground.
Two points for each correct word.

SPOT IN THE PICTURE
One point for finding each of the things asked for.

Record your total score for pages 50-51.

PAGES 52-53

BRAIN TEASER
The master said exactly the same words to the two servants. So there were no differences.
Five points for correct answer.

REACH FOR YOUR CALCULATOR

a: 33 (5+5+5+5+2+2+2+2=33)
b: 10   c: 4
Three points for each correct answer.

CHECK IT OUT!
Five points for reading this, or listening as it is read to you.

WHO'S WHO?
1b; 2a; 3a

SPOT IN THE PICTURE
One point for finding each of the things asked for.

Record your total score for pages 52-53.

PAGES 54-55

BRAIN TEASER
Master, father, ground, people, afraid, should.
Two points for each correct word.

MAKE A LIST
One point for each thing on your list, up to ten points.

CHECK IT OUT!
Five points for reading this, or listening as it is read to you.

ACTIVITY TIME
One point for each word not linked to the story, up to a maximum of five points.
Five points for each word, such as 'bank', found in the story.

SPOT IN THE PICTURE
One point for finding each of the things asked for.

Record your total score for pages 54-55.

Add up and record your total score for the story about using your talents.

PAGES 56-57

CLOCKWORDS
a: PRAY   b: NAME   c: EACH
d: HOLY   e: FOOD
Three points for each correct word.

ACTIVITY TIME
Ten points.

CHECK IT OUT!
Five points for reading this, or listening as it is read to you.

BRAIN TEASER
Continue to **ask**, and God will give to you. **Continue** to **search**, and you will **find**. **Begin** to **knock**, and the **door** will **open** for you.
One point for each correct word.

SPOT IN THE PICTURE
One point for finding each of the things asked for.

Record your total score for pages 56-57.

PAGES 58-59

BRAIN TEASER
He wanted to eat only the small pieces of food that fell from the rich man's table.
Five points.

QUIZ
1b; 2 We are not told the name of the rich man.
Three points for each correct answer.

CHECK IT OUT!
Five points for reading this, or listening as it is read to you.

DRAW
Five points for the drawing.
Five points for coloring or painting it.

SPOT IN THE PICTURE
One point for finding each of the things asked for.

Record your total score for pages 58-59.

PAGES 60-61

WORD SEARCH
They have the law of Moses and the writings.
One point for each correct word.
Abraham.
Five points.

BRAIN TEASER
All the words can be made into other words by adding the letter 's' in front of them.
Sin, sand, scan, son
Ten points.

CHECK IT OUT!
Five points for reading this, or listening as it is read to you.

QUIZ
a: Five
b: The prophets, or Moses, or the Old Testament, or, the Bible.
Three points for a correct answer.

SPOT IN THE PICTURE
One point for finding each of the things asked for.

Record your total score for pages 60-61.

Add up and record your total score for the story of the rich man and Lazarus.

Add up your total score for the whole book.

Faith Builder Guide

New Testament
Activity Bible

Age: 8-12

Life Issue: Learning to have faith in God,
no matter what the circumstances

Spiritual Building Block: Faith

Learning Styles

Help your child learn about faith in the following ways:

Sight: Watch a story video about any of the stories in this book with a friend. Talk about what the story means and try to think of examples in your everyday life where the same principles apply. How can your faith in God help you to make the right choices?

Sound: Read the stories aloud to a group of friends or to your younger sister or brother. Why do you think Jesus used stories to teach a principle? Think of an example in your life that closely matches one of the stories in this book. Were the decisions that you made in that situation good ones? What was the result?

Touch: Choose one or two of the stories in this book and create a play with your friends. "The Boy Who Left Home" is a good choice because you can add a lot of action. Review the story so that you have it clearly in your mind. Then look for some simple costumes in a closet or old clothes box. Check with your Mom or Dad to make sure it is OK to use the items you have selected. The story will come alive as you become one of the characters. Have fun and enjoy learning about God's Word with your friends.